Fibres in Fashion

Sally Cowan

NELSON
CENGAGE Learning

Australia • Brazil • Japan • Korea • Mexico • Singapore • Spain • United Kingdom • United States

NELSON
CENGAGE Learning™

Fibres in Fashion

Text: Sally Cowan
Designer: Sonia Young
Editor: Anna McKenna
Illustrations: Virginia Grey and John Taylor
Photographs: Bill Thomas and Lindsay Edwards
Typeset in Legacy Sans

Acknowledgements
AAP Image, pp. 5, 27 top; Advertising Archive Ltd, p. 24 top right; ANT Photo Library/NHPA pp. 16 bottom, 9 bottom; Australian Picture Library/Corbis/Pablo Corral, p. 5 top /Anthony Bannister, p. 6 top right /Leigh Snider, p. 6 bottom right /Danny Lehman, p. 7 bottom /Brian A. Vikander, p. 9 and cover /Michael S. Yamashita, p. 10 bottom /Jack Fields, p. 11 top /The State Hermitage Museum, St Petersburg, Russia, p. 16 top /Nevada Wier, p. 18 top /Charles & Josette Lenars, p. 20 bottom /John Madere, p. 23 top /Reuter Raymond, p. 23 bottom /Iundt Dimitri, p. 26 /Vittoriano Rastelli, p. 28 top left /Jacques M. Chenet, p. 30 bottom; Bill Thomas, pp. 8 right and cover, 12 right and cover, 25 bottom left, 28 bottom, back cover (hat); Corbis, p. 13; Getty Images/Taxi, p. 7 top /Hulton Archive, p. 24 right; Image Addict, p. 25 bottom right; Lindsay Edwards, pp. 1, 2-3, 20-21 (background), 30-31 (background and plastic bags); PhotoDisc, pp. 8 top left, 11 bottom, 21 bottom; photolibrary.com/SPL, p. 12 top left /Rick Strange, p. 19 /Mikael Dubois, p. 21 top /SuperStock, pp. 24 bottom right, 25 top right, 25 centre right /Penny Tweedie, p. 30 top; Picture Source/Terry Oakley, p.22 left and right; Stock Photos, pp. 27 bottom, 28 top right /Lance Nelson, pp. 6 top left, 6 centre, 10 top /Masterfile/Brian Sytnyk, pp.6 centre right, 20 top /John Oxley Library, p. 8 bottom left; The Art Archive/Musee du Louvre Paris/Dagli Orti, p. 4 left.

PM Plus Non Fiction
Sapphire
Colour Around Us
The Science of cooking
Fibres in Fashion
Making Shapes
Built Like That
Measure for Measure

For product information and technology assistance,
in Australia call 1300 790 853;
in New Zealand call 0508 635 766

For permission to use material from this text or product,
please email **aust.permissions@cengage.com**

ISBN 978 0 17 009945 5
ISBN 978 0 17 009939 4 (set)

Cengage Learning Australia
Level 7, 80 Dorcas Street
South Melbourne, Victoria Australia 3205

Cengage Learning New Zealand
Unit 4B Rosedale Office Park
331 Rosedale Road, Albany, North Shore NZ 0632

For learning solutions, visit **cengage.com.au**

Printed in China by 1010 Printing International Ltd
9 10 13 12

Contents

Chapter 1

Clothes from Fibres

Most clothes we wear are made from fibres. There are **natural** fibres, and **synthetic** fibres, which are made from chemicals.

Before people discovered natural fibres, they wore clothes made from grasses, leaves, animal furs and skins. They used fringing, shells and beads of ivory and bone to make their clothes more attractive. This was the start of **fashion**.

As civilisations developed, people learned new **technologies** for making clothes. They discovered how to take fibres from some plants and animals, and spin and weave them to make cloth.

This 4 000-year-old plaque from Mesopotamia shows a woman weaving.

Today, fibres and fashion are huge industries. Factories make vast amounts of cloth from natural fibres to make our clothes. They also make cloth from synthetic fibres. Scientists invented these fibres to provide cheaper cloth for the growing population of the world. They also wanted to make substitutes for some of the more luxurious natural fibres that were expensive to produce.

A textile worker watches as a mechanical loom weaves fabric.

Synthetic fibre technology has become so advanced that there are now fibres for making clothes for special purposes, such as helping athletes to run or swim faster and keeping police officers safe.

New inventions in fibre technology continue to change the fashions we wear.

Chapter 2

Natural Fibres

Natural fibres come from plants and animals. The most popular natural fibres are cotton, wool, silk and linen. They have been used to make clothes for centuries.

Natural fibres come from these plants and animals.

The fibres must be **processed** before they are turned into clothes. They are washed and put through special machines that separate any tangles. Then the fibres are twisted and spun together to form long, strong **yarn**. In the past, spinning was done by hand on a spinning wheel, but today large machines spin the yarn.

A spinning wheel

The yarn can be woven or knitted to make cloth, which is also called fabric. Yarn is woven on large machines called looms, or knitted on knitting machines. The machines use the latest computer technology to make thousands of metres of fabric quickly and efficiently.

A large loom in a factory

A woman in Mexico weaving on a traditional loom

Did you know?
In some parts of the world, people still weave fabric on traditional handlooms.

Cotton

Cotton grows on plants. People like to wear cotton clothing because it 'breathes'. This means it does not hold heat close to the body, so it is cool to wear in hot weather.

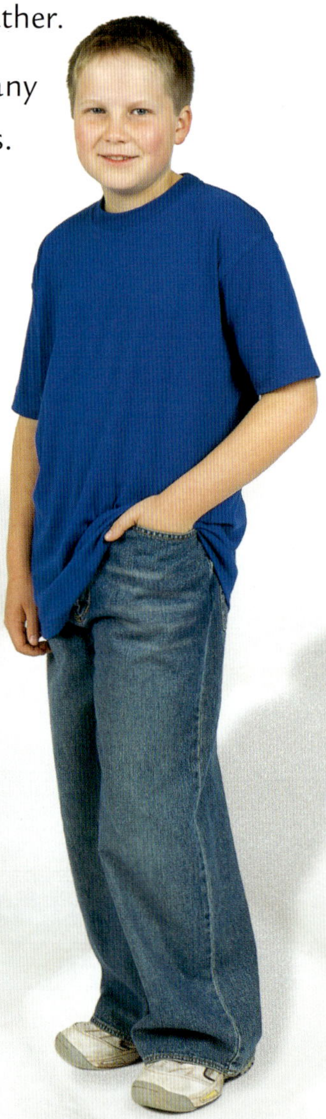

Cotton fibres are made into many different fabrics and all sorts of fashion styles. What are you wearing today – jeans, shorts, a t-shirt, or button-front shirt? It is likely that something you are wearing is made of cotton.

Jeans are made from a strong cotton fabric called denim.

The first jeans were made in the 1870s and were hard-wearing pants for workers. Denim jeans became fashionable about 100 years later and are still popular today.

Cotton is one of the oldest fibres used for making clothes. It was first grown in ancient India. Archaeologists have found cotton cloth in Pakistan that is about 5000 years old.

Cotton was introduced to Western countries about 500 years ago.

Indian women have worn colourful cotton saris like this for thousands of years.

Fibre fact

In the Middle Ages, an English explorer returning from India described the cotton plant he had seen as a 'wonderful tree which bore tiny lambs on the end of its branches'.

Cotton farming

The cotton plant grows flowers that wither away and leave bolls. Bolls contain many seeds. When the seeds are ripe, the **bolls** burst open, revealing fluffy balls of cotton fibres.

In the past, cotton was picked by hand, which took a long time. Today, farmers use large harvester machines to collect the cotton.

The cotton must be cleaned of any seeds or leaves, and then pressed tightly into bags called **bales**. The bales of cotton are taken to a **mill** where they are put into machines that spin the fibres into a strong yarn. The yarn is then ready to be dyed and made into fabric.

This machine is spinning cotton.

The future of cotton

Scientists are developing new kinds of cotton plants using **genetic engineering** to change the plants. They want to make the plants stronger and more **resistant** to pests, so that farmers will not need to spray their crops with insecticides.

A cropdusting plane spraying cotton

Scientists want to develop cotton plants that need less water and can grow during droughts. They also want to improve the quality of the cotton fibres by making them resistant to fire and less likely to wrinkle. They even hope to grow coloured cotton, so that it will not need to be dyed!

Could this be what cotton crops will look like in the future?

Wool

Wool comes from sheep. Wool is popular for making clothes because it is soft and warm to wear. Like cotton, it can be made into many different fabrics. Woollen clothing can be smooth and fine or big and bulky. Take a look at the clothes in the shops near you – all sorts of woollen garments are in fashion.

A wool fibre seen under a microscope.

A wool fibre is finer than a strand of human hair, and it has many special qualities that make it suitable for clothing.

Each fibre is covered in tiny scales that make it soft, yet strong. The fibres are **crimped** and trap air next to our bodies. The air heats up and keeps us warm. Wool **absorbs** moisture from the air, so it is slow to catch fire and safe to wear. It can also absorb dyes more easily than some plant fibres.

Fibre fact

Wool fibres are covered in a kind of grease, which is collected and purified to make lanolin. Lanolin is used in soap and cosmetics.

Sheep farming

In ancient times, wild sheep lived in cold, mountainous places. They grew thick **fleeces**. The outer layer of wool was coarse and tough, while the layer underneath was soft and thick to keep the animals warm.

People began to keep flocks of sheep more than 6000 years ago. They learned how to spin the fibres and weave them to make cloth. This was a big advance in civilisation because people no longer needed to hunt wild animals for food and clothing. They did not have to kill the sheep to use the wool: they plucked it from the sheep by hand.

Since then, people have bred sheep to improve their fleeces. Today farmers keep huge flocks of sheep for producing wool, and there are many breeds of sheep with different kinds of wool. The finest fleeces come from Merino sheep.

Fibre fact

Australia is the world's biggest producer of Merino wool. New Zealand, South Africa and Argentina also produce a lot of wool.

From sheep to shop

At the wool shed

Shearers use electric clippers to shear the sheep. Skilled shearers work fast, shearing about 150 sheep a day. The wool shorn in one piece from a sheep is called a fleece.

Did you know?

Shearing doesn't hurt the sheep – it's just like having a haircut!

The wool is packed into tight bales by a special pressing machine. Then the bales are sold to wool factories.

At the wool factory

The wool is washed, then combed and brushed in a machine that separates the tangled fibres. The fibres are then spun into yarn to be woven or knitted to make fabric.

At the clothing factory

The fabric is cut and sewn to make the latest fashions.

At the wool shop

Some yarn is also sent to shops to be sold for knitting at home.

Many people like to knit.
They can create their own fashions.

Fibre fact

People also use the wool of several other animals, including goats, llamas and rabbits.

Silk

Silk comes from silkworms. Silk clothing is very comfortable, because it is cool to wear in summer and can be warm in winter. Silk has been fashionable for thousands of years because it can be made into rich fabrics that look beautiful and feel soft and smooth.

The Chinese discovered how to make silk from the long, **lustrous** fibre of silkworm cocoons. For a long time the Chinese kept the method of making silk a secret from the rest of the world.

A 19th-century French dress made of silk and velvet.

Silkworms are actually caterpillars, not worms.

Fibre fact

Silkworms that feed on the leaves of the white mulberry tree produce the finest silk.

By around AD 300, Japan and India had also discovered how to make silk, and merchants sold it to the Romans and Greeks. Silk became very fashionable and was worn by only the wealthiest people, such as Roman emperors and officials. For hundreds of years, fine silks were traded from the East to the West along the trade route known as the Silk Road.

The Silk Road stretched from China to Italy.

Eventually the secret got out to Europe, and big silk industries developed, first in Italy and then in France. By the 1600s, huge silk looms wove beautiful fabrics that only kings, queens and wealthy people could afford. These clothes were much desired.

Silkworm farming

Silkworm moths lay eggs, which hatch as silkworms. Silkworm farms contain rows and rows of thousands of caterpillars, all feeding on mulberry leaves.

Feeding silkworms at a silkworm farm

When a silkworm is about six weeks old, it produces one long fibre from its body, which it spins around itself to form a cocoon. The fibre is very strong and much longer than any of the other natural fibres. A single fibre from a cocoon can be up to 1000 metres long.

A silkworm cocoon

At a factory, the cocoons are softened in hot water. The end of the silk fibre is found and the fibres of several cocoons are unwound and twisted together to make a strong thread. The yarn is then dyed and woven into silk fabric.

silk tie

Fibre fact

It takes about 110 cocoons to make a silk tie.

Linen

Linen comes from the flax plant. The long, thin stems are soaked in water so that the fibres inside can be separated from the plant. They are dried, then combed straight to make long, strong fibres.

Linen has been a fashionable fibre since the time of the ancient Egyptians. The Pharaohs and other wealthy people wore long flowing robes of fine linen, while workers wore heavier linen loincloths or simple dresses.

Linen creases easily, and **pleating** became fashionable with wealthy Egyptians. After washing, they sent their wet clothes to a pleater, who folded them into small even pleats, tied them tightly and hung them out to dry.

Linen fibres are harder to dye than cotton and wool, so most of the ancient Egyptians' clothes were white.

Linen is often used in home furnishings

Linen was cool to wear in the hot Egyptian climate. Today it is still fashionable to wear linen in summer. However, linen is expensive to produce and there are now synthetic fibres that look like linen, but do not crease and are cheaper to produce.

Because it is so strong, linen has also been used for making tablecloths, tea towels, curtains and furniture coverings.

Fibre fact

Jute plants are similar to flax plants, but produce much thicker fibres. They are used for making rope, string, sacks and carpets.

Chapter 3

Synthetic Fibres

People make synthetic fibres using chemicals. Scientists first experimented with synthetic fibres so they could make lots of fabric cheaply. They wanted the fabrics to look like they were made from natural fibres.

How synthetic fibres are made

1. **The chemicals are melted in vats to make a hot, thick plastic liquid.**

2. **The liquid is forced through many small holes in a spinneret, similar to the way that water comes out of a showerhead. When it leaves the spinneret, the plastic makes long, stringy fibres.**

Fibre fact

Unlike natural fibres, synthetic fibres can be made into different thicknesses by changing the size of the holes in the spinneret.

3

The fibres are dried and stretched to make long **continuous strands.**

4

Like natural fibres, synthetic fibres are twisted to make yarn, and sent to factories to be woven or knitted into fabric.

Synthetic fibres in fashion

The invention of synthetic fibres has changed the fashions we wear.

1935 First synthetic fibre

Nylon was the first synthetic fibre to be invented. Long, continuous nylon fibres are very fine, smooth, silky, stretchy and strong. By the 1940s, women wore nylon stockings, which were much cheaper than the original silk stockings. Nylon could be woven tightly and was strong enough to make parachutes.

An old advertisement for nylon stockings

1950s and 1960s Easy-care clothes

Scientists developed synthetic fibres that were soft, warm, easy to wash and quick to dry. The fibres did not crease, so clothes did not need ironing, and they could be dyed bright colours. Fashions changed as people wore the bright new colours in everyday clothes.

1970s Back to nature

Many of the early synthetic fabrics, such as polyester and nylon, were uncomfortable to wear because they did not let air circulate around the body. People got very hot and sweaty wearing them. During this time, natural fibres became fashionable again.

1980s Fibres for fun and fitness

Fibre technology kept up with the fashion for fitness, health and exercise. A super-stretchy fibre called Lycra became fashionable as people needed special clothes for exercising. They wanted to look good in clothes that could stretch and hug the body to fit perfectly. Large sports clothing **manufacturers** began to spend millions of dollars on research into developing special clothes for sporting activities.

1990s Fibres from rubbish

New technology meant that plastic bottles could be melted down and made into fibres for clothing. Polar fleece is made from recycled plastic bottles. It is soft and very warm. It became fashionable with people of all ages.

It's hard to believe that this vest is made from plastic bottles!

Today

Fibres that were once only used for fitness clothing are now popular in everyday clothing because they are comfortable and look good. Big sports clothing manufacturers continue to invent new fibres that will change the fashions we wear.

Chapter 4

Special Purpose Fibres

Scientists have developed other synthetic fibres such as very fine **microfibres** that 'breathe' and draw heat and sweat away from the body. These fibres are used to make clothes specially designed for all kinds of sports including running, tennis, soccer and swimming.

Athletes may run faster with new fibre technology

More than two years of research has gone into making a special running suit designed to help athletes run faster. The suit is made using the latest in fibre technology. Some parts of the suit have heavy fabric to keep muscles warm, while other parts have lighter 'breathable' fabric to keep the athlete cool.

Textured fabrics are used in some parts of the suit and the **seams** are located at the back. These features are designed to cut down on **wind drag** so the athlete can run faster.

Many athletes are very excited about the new suits and will be wearing them at sporting competitions around the world.

Fibres for protection

Bulletproof vests are made from a synthetic fibre that is stronger than steel. The fibre is also used to make protective clothing for logging workers to prevent chainsaw cuts.

More recently, scientists have been working on new ways of producing spider silk. Spiders make different types of silk, and the silk used in their webs is one of the strongest natural fibres in the world.

A police officer wearing a bulletproof vest

Fibre fact

Scientists believe that a bundle of spider silk as thick as a pencil would be strong enough to stop a flying jumbo jet.

Unlike silkworms, spiders are aggressive towards each other so it is difficult to keep spiders and farm their webs. Scientists are working on other ways to make large amounts of spider silk using genetic engineering. They hope that the fibre will be used for protective clothing, such as bulletproof vests, and that it will be even stronger and lighter than the synthetic fibres used today.

Special synthetic fibre suits provide protection for racing car drivers. Racing is a dangerous sport where crashes sometimes cause fires. The suits are easy to move in, cool to wear and slow to catch fire.

Firefighters wear special uniforms that protect them from fire and chemicals.

We can also wear protective clothing to stop us from getting sunburnt. The clothes are comfortable to wear because they stretch with the body and dry quickly.

Sun protection clothing helps prevent sunburn and skin cancer.

Clothes with sun protection are now a part of everyday life.

School News

Notice to students and parents: Sports uniform update

Our school has had the same sports uniform for the past 12 years. Over that time there have been many developments and improvements in fabrics. We have researched some of the fabrics and decided to make these changes.

1. The new tracksuit will be made from a microfibre fabric, which is very comfortable to wear and easy to wash and dry.
2. The sports top and shorts will be made from a new fabric that has just come onto the market. It wears well, is comfortable and has in-built **SPF** 50+ sun protection.

The new sports uniform will be available to buy next term.

Chapter 5

A Smart Future

There will probably always be a place for natural fibres in fashion. They are still fashionable today after thousands of years, and some clothes have hardly changed since ancient times.

These men in modern-day Morocco, Africa, are wearing traditional clothing.

However, scientists have invented new fibres, so that today we have some of the most comfortable and practical clothes ever.

Our ancestors wore real furs to keep warm. Today, people can wear clothes made from fake fur fibres that look just like the real thing.

In the future we may wear 'smart' clothes that can do things for us. Scientists are trying to make fibres that work like solar panels, generating electricity when out in the sunshine. We could use our clothes to recharge a portable phone or computer. Imagine how practical that could be! It may soon be possible to press a button to change the colour of our clothes.

Perhaps we will use more recycling to make new fibres. Some fashion designers think that fabrics made from recycled plastic shopping bags will be widely used.

Who knows what we'll be wearing in the future?

Glossary

absorbs	soaks up moisture
bales	large bundles or bags
bolls	hard case on a cotton plant containing the seeds
continuous	goes on and on without a break
crimped	containing small ridges
fashion	styles of clothing that are popular at a particular time
fleeces	coats of wool
genetic engineering	scientific process to change genes
lustrous	smooth, bright and shining
manufacturers	companies that produce goods
microfibres	very fine synthetic fibres
mill	a place where fibres are taken to be processed
natural	from nature
pleating	folding fabric to make even ridges
processed	changed by treatments in a factory
resistant	able to stop something from happening
seams	joins where pieces of fabric are sewn together in clothes
SPF	'sun protection factor'
spinneret	something that hot plastic flows through to form fibres
strands	very thin long pieces, like threads
synthetic	made by people
technologies	methods of making things using tools and machinery
wind drag	resistance from the wind while running
yarn	fibres that have been spun and are ready to use